Beautiful
Britain
Plantagenet Somerset Fry

This edition produced exclusively for

WHSMITH

Designed by Groom and Pickerill

Photography by Tony Stone Associates
Front jacket: Henley-on-Thames, Oxfordshire
Back jacket: Stob Ghablar and Clack Leathad Mountains, Strathclyde, Scotland
Endpapers: Cullin Hills, Isle of Skye
Title spread: Dartmoor, Devon

**This edition published exclusively for
W H Smith**

Published by
The Hamlyn Publishing Group Limited
London·New York·Sydney·Toronto
Astronaut House, Feltham, Middlesex, England

Copyright © The Hamlyn Publishing Group Limited 1981
ISBN 0 600 37661 3

Printed in Italy

CONTENTS

Introduction

All countries are beautiful to their inhabitants. Each has something unique to offer to visitors and has a history which its people recall with pride and warmth. What, then, is so special about Britain?

Nowhere in Britain is there the kind of breathtaking scenery such as you find in Kenya or Kashmir. It has no splendid ancient buildings like the Pyramids of Egypt or the Parthenon in Athens. There are no huge rivers like the Amazon in South America or the Missouri-Mississippi in the United States, nor mountains like the Himalayas, nor deserts like the Gobi. Civilization reached Britain less than 4,000 years ago, which is late in the human time scale, and its early development had no significant influence upon the progress of mankind. In world geographical terms it is a small place and it goes nowhere. To get to it you have to make a special journey across the sea. Like all other countries, its history has been shaped by its geography as much as by anything else, and in turn its history has moulded its landscape. Yet more people visit Britain than almost anywhere else in the world, while for centuries it has been somewhere to which peoples of other nations have come to settle. ·

Britain, which is only a twelfth of the area of the state of Texas in the U.S.A., packs into its very small space an astonishing variety: cathedrals of every period in 900 years of building history, ancient monuments by the hundred, some reaching back to the 3rd millennium B.C., castles by the thousand, churches by the ten thousand, old homes, great and small, by the hundred thousand. They are scattered about in numerous counties and districts in the four countries England, Wales, Scotland and Northern Ireland that make up Britain, and also in the Republic of Ireland, or Eire. And they are for the most part linked by the best and most diffuse road system anywhere. Each of the many counties and districts is different from the next and the differences are instantly noticeable, whether in the type of stone used for building, or the style of country or village cottage, or even by the accent with which the English language is pronounced by the locals. Added to that, Wales, Scotland and the Irish Republic have their own native tongues, branches of the Celtic group of languages, and people of Cornwall and the Isle of Man also speak their own Celtic tongues.

These are perhaps the outward and visible signs that fascinate the visitor. There are less tangible aspects of Britain that make it remarkable. It has not been invaded from Europe or anywhere else for over 900 years. It is the home of the Mother of Parliaments. It was the first country in the world to be industrialised. It once ruled the greatest empire the world has ever seen, which covered a quarter of the land on the surface of the earth. Its territorial power has gone, but paradoxically its spiritual influence is greater than ever. Above all, its people and its institutions appear to be indestructible.

Fiona and Plantagenet Somerset Fry

Counties and Regions of the British Isles

Historic Counties of the British Isles

CL — CLACKMANNANSHIRE
DUN — DUNBARTONSHIRE
KIN — KINROSS-SHIRE

England

London and the South East

Few countries can boast so impressive a monument at its entrance as Dover Castle. The first landmark visitors see when they come across the English Channel from France, Dover Castle, mediaeval upon Roman remains, massive, fortified and used for almost nine centuries, stands guard upon the British Isles as if to say, 'If you come in peace, welcome! If you come armed for war, beware!' Down below the castle's tremendous walls and towers lies the bustling port town. Once a Roman port, next a fortified Saxon town, then a Norman base, a Cinque Port of the Middle Ages, and finally the main centre of the Channel coast defence system, Dover handles an ever-growing volume of traffic, with ships and hovercraft to and from France and Belgium, trains direct to the capital, London, and fast roads into England. One of these, Watling Street, was begun by the Romans nearly 1,900 years ago, and extended right into North Wales.

Dover is the gateway to Kent, the Garden of England. In the north of the county Kent is divided east and west by the River Medway—the river up which the Dutch admiral de Ruyter triumphantly sailed in 1667—with its naval dockyard at Chatham, its cathedral town and castle of Rochester. The north and south of the county are divided by the chalk hills of the North Downs which Winston Churchill loved and where he made his home, at Chartwell on the edge of the Downs. To the south of Chartwell spreads the great Weald of Kent, once light woodland, famous for its charcoal for iron-making, now fertile and prosperous from hop-growing, dairy farming and fruit orchards. Perhaps Kent's most famous town is Canterbury, where St. Augustine founded the English Church in 597, and where the Normans built a great cathedral. It was in this cathedral that Archbishop Thomas Becket was murdered in 1170. His shrine remains a place of pilgrimage for Christians even today.

This fine mosaic floor (*above*) was laid within the six-acre Roman palace at Fishbourne, Sussex during the 3rd century A.D. A winged boy sits astride a dolphin, surrounded by sea-horses and sea-panthers.

The tremendous walls and towers of Dover Castle (*left*) have protected the entrance to England for eight centuries. William the Conqueror raised a motte-and-bailey over existing Iron Age earthworks and Henry II and his son King John built the great stone castle.

Lying alongside Kent is East and West Sussex. Sussex, *Suth Seaxe*, was the kingdom of the south Saxons led by tough Aelle who landed at Pevensey in 477, a few miles from the beachhead established almost 600 years later by William the Bastard, the Conqueror or whatever else the defeated Anglo-Saxons called him. The Romans liked Sussex, with its cliffs, its South Downs and its woods, or they would not have covered its plains with villas like Bignor and Fishbourne. Iron Age Celts preferred the higher ground and built forts like Cissbury and Chanctonbury Ring in West Sussex. From Chanctonbury on a clear day you can see 'the London of the South', Brighton. First called Brighthelmstone, it was once a fishing village and then a health resort for gouty 18th-century politicians and rakes, which the Prince Regent, eldest son of George III, preferred to London. Here, Henry Holland built for him the fairytale Pavilion in Moorish style, and John Nash, a generation later, re-created it for him in oriental style.

Some 55 miles due north of Brighton is London. Travelling to it you must go out of Sussex and through Surrey, with its gentle,

Massive Windsor Castle, the most ancient of
the royal residences, extends for half a mile
along the hill above the little town of
Windsor. In the background to the right is
the King Edward III Tower and to the left the
Round Tower.

Hampton Court was built by Thomas Wolsey who in 1526 offered it to Henry VIII in a bid to regain the King's favour. It remained a royal residence until 1760.

undulating woodland and chalk hills, its rich fields, its Sunday-afternoon-in-the-country resorts of Boxhill and Leith Hill for tired Londoners, and Sir Edward Maufe's magnificent 20th-century Guildford Cathedral which overlooks the famous Hog's Back to Farnham and its castle. To the north of the county, in Greater London, is one of the finest royal houses in England, Hampton Court.

Edmund Spenser's 'sweet Thames', England's second longest river (210 miles to the Severn's 220), winds through the north of Surrey. The Thames is also Berkshire's northern edge, flowing past Windsor Castle which Duke William (the Conqueror) began in 1067 by scarping a mound out of a chalk cliff by the river. Berkshire is noted for its fine agricultural fields, pigs, forests and heaths, golf courses and race tracks, and for Maidenhead, on the Thames, whose elegant riverside hotels, restaurants and houses reflect the carefree and spendthrift lives of the Edwardians who built most of them.

Eastwards from Berkshire is an area of Greater London once known as Middlesex, so called because it was a kind of buffer district between East and West Saxons.

Recently the area has been thought of as one with drab houses, untidy gas and water works, and sprawling factories, but its many fine houses should not be overlooked, among them Syon House in Isleworth, Chiswick House, one of the grandest Palladian-style homes in the country, and a host of later and lesser homes built sturdily and with considerable originality of design, many of them between the two World Wars.

'At length they all to merry London came', wrote the poet Spenser, in *Prothalamion*, towards the end of the great Virgin Queen's reign, and still they come today . . .

London, capital city of Great Britain, once the centre of a great

This imposing building, on the site of what was originally James I's mulberry orchard, was built by the Duke of Buckingham and Chandos, sold to George III in 1761 and is now the London residence of the royal family. The statue before Buckingham Palace, the Winged Victory, was erected as a monument to Queen Victoria.

For two thousand years, the waterways of England transported heavy commercial cargoes. Now they mainly carry pleasure craft and every year, more than 23,000 small boats pass through Boulter's Lock, Maidenhead (*right*), the longest and deepest of the Thames locks.

This windmill in Shipley, Sussex, which belonged to the writer Hilaire Belloc, is of a type known as a smock mill, a name earned because the white painted weatherboarding looks like a countryman's smock.

empire and today still a formidable influence, is a vast city spreading along both sides of the Thames. Its multitudes of landmarks are instantly visible to travellers over the many river bridges or wanderers across the heights of Hampstead, Highgate or Sydenham: Wren's masterpiece of St. Paul's Cathedral, boldly projecting among the many shapeless monoliths of 20th-century office requirements, Big Ben with its bell that comforted millions during the dark years of war with Hitler, the White Tower of London, over 90 feet tall and still a symbol of Britain's remarkable history, and Nelson's Column in Trafalgar Square, a reminder that Britain once ruled the waves. These and the many other famous landmarks draw vast crowds, year after year to the capital, but perhaps none more so than Buckingham Palace, London home of the first family in the land.

England

East Anglia

North out of the capital, three main roads run. The Great North Road (A1) and the A10 push deep into the lovely undulating countryside of Hertfordshire and carve their way into Cambridgeshire, a county enlarged since 1974 to include historic Huntingdonshire. The third road, the M11 runs through Essex, its countryside graced by Epping Forest, once the hunting playground of kings. These fine highways, two of them of Roman origin, skirt the western edge of East Anglia, that unique part of England which bulges into the North Sea. First limited to Norfolk and Suffolk, it now more generally includes Cambridgeshire, parts of Hertfordshire, Essex, Bedfordshire with its glorious hills and valleys and the stately home of the Duke of Bedford, Woburn Abbey, and Northamptonshire, county of

stone quarries and shoemakers.

Cambridgeshire, whose fenlands, criss-crossed by drainage canals, make it one of the most productive farming parts of the country, has in its county town Cambridge the second oldest English university, housed in 27 residential colleges. Many of them are of mediaeval beginnings and among the finest buildings of that kind anywhere in northern Europe. Take a boat or punt down the River Cam along what are world-famous as The Backs and see Henry VI's King's College Chapel with its astonishing fan-vaulted roof, or the library at Trinity designed by Christopher Wren, who charged no fees. Here in Cambridge, scholars and townsfolk have since the 12th century tried, sometimes not very successfully, to live harmoniously, following totally different walks of life.

(*Overleaf.*) The lovely 17th-century cottages at Arkesden, Essex, are a reminder of a highly-skilled art, that of the thatcher. A stout timber frame supports the lath and plaster walls.

The famous Bridge of Sighs in Venice was the model for this carved stone footbridge (*below*) which crosses the River Cam from the wide lawns and willow trees of the Cambridge Backs to St. John's College, a Tudor foundation.

To the south and east of the city lie the East Anglian Heights and the borders between Cambridgeshire, Essex and Suffolk. Essex can be proud of its picturesque half-timbered cottages, thatch-roofed and tiled, its fertile curving countryside with very narrow lanes and high-banked fields. Yet, because of its fertility hedges have been ripped out by farmers anxious to force the last yard of earth under the plough. On down through the county, stop and savour the charming market town of Saffron Walden, whose pretty name comes from its local growing of saffron crocuses up to the 1800s. Then six miles south, curve your way through Thaxted, with its famous guildhall and its large church once destined to be an Essex cathedral, whose living was once in the gift of Edward VII's left-wing mistress, the Countess of Warwick. Southwards to Chelmsford, stopping place for Boudicca's victorious army that had just burned Colchester and was heading for London and St. Albans to do the same. Continue south to the Thames estuary with its long, squiggly coastline

with havens for all kinds of boats. Jutting into the estuary at Southend is the pier, a wonderful ribbon of pleasure over a mile long and now threatened with demolition. To the north-east of Southend is Colchester, one of Rome's first colonies, built next to the capital of Cunobelinus (Shakespeare's Cymbeline), king of the Belgic Catuvellauni who lorded it over most of southern Britain before the arrival of Emperor Claudius's legions in A.D. 43. Nearby is Colchester Castle, the biggest of the mediaeval great towers and one of the very earliest, put up by the Conqueror to fight off sea attack.

North of Essex is Suffolk, the two counties having a natural border, the River Stour. Suffolk was land of the South Folk, one of the branches of Angles to settle on the eastern side of Britain when proud Rome bent before the hordes of Goth and Vandal, Visigoth and Hun, and pulled her troops away from the island. The county, whose lush foliage, majestic oak trees and endlessly rolling hills foster the natural warmth of the people, gave birth to Constable (East

Bergholt), Gainsborough (Sudbury), Cardinal Wolsey (Ipswich) and Benjamin Britten (Lowestoft). Its county town Ipswich has little to recommend it now that planners have spoiled its heart, but follow the road which runs alongside the River Orwell to the north-west and it will lead to Bury St. Edmunds, one of England's most beautiful towns, site of one of the biggest Benedictine abbeys whose ruins, little more than fragments, are gloriously set in spacious gardens lovingly tended by a sensitive local authority.

Suffolk's north-eastern edge is on the River Waveney, and across that you come into Norfolk, a colder county in climate, its people vigorous, hard-working and fiercely independent like their ancestors, the North Folk Angles. The cradle of British agriculture, where many innovations of the Agrarian Revolution stemmed—Coke who converted West Norfolk from rye to wheat growing, Townshend who introduced planted grasses and turnip crops and demonstrated crop rotation—Norfolk's wealth from

Racehorses going down to the start before a race give the punters a final chance to check form. Newmarket boasts the roots of British racing from the days when Charles II used to race his horses on the Heath. Since then, this small Suffolk town has developed into the centre of a thriving racehorse industry.

When Suffolk was rich in oak forests, many of the county's houses and cottages were oak-framed. Lavenham, which prospered as a centre of the Tudor wool trade, has preserved its timbered houses; in some, weathered oak studs are exposed to the street, the old walls of others — colour-washed pink, blue, cream or buff — lean at all angles as the timbers have become warped and bowed with time.

land and its yields is reflected, as nowhere else in Britain, in its houses. The county abounds in medium-sized mansions, fit for lords of the manor anywhere else but in fact built for well-established farmers. Norwich, a fine city, and still almost unspoiled, has a matchless Norman cathedral, tall-spired, cryptless, with one of the longest naves in Britain, and a Norman castle restored by the Victorian architect, Salvin. The city bristles with the independence it showed in mediaeval times when its mayor spoke to Southampton's as England spoke to France. Private banks and a building society, the only provincial theatre that makes money, a unique covered market—these are the kind of enterprises that ensure the city could exist on its own without the rest of the country.

North and east are the famous Broads, a series of inland lakes surrounded by flat fields and linked by streams and rivers with charming villages alongside their banks. To the west are the rich lands reclaimed from the Wash, and King's Lynn, famous as one of England's largest mediaeval ports, still bustling with more recent industry and carefully preserving its many old buildings.

Two rivers empty into the Wash, the Great Ouse on which stands the tiny Cambridgeshire city of Ely, dominated by the huge cathedral with its landmark octagon tower that can be seen from miles around, and the River Nene, beside which lies the cathedral city of Peterborough on the margin of the Fens.

A peaceful scene on the River Bure at Horning (*above*). Every summer, thousands of boating enthusiasts visit the Norfolk Broads, where 200 miles of waterways link shallow lakes which were once ancient peat diggings, and wild life flourishes.

In past centuries, the gentry of Norfolk often kept town houses in Norwich, where they could bring their families for balls and entertainments. These fine Georgian houses (*right*) are in Tombland – a name which has nothing to do with tombs but refers to an ancient Saxon market.

England

The Chilterns and Cotswolds

Around the beautiful Chiltern and Cotswold hills lies a cluster of south Midland counties, all blessed with marvellous countryside with something different round every corner. These are the shires of Buckingham and Oxford, through which the chalky Chiltern Hills wind, of Northampton and Warwick, rolling hills and dales for hunting, interspersed with great centres of industry and population, of Gloucester, dominated by the Cotswolds whose greybrown limestone spills out into buildings of village and town, and of Worcester and Hereford, nestling under the protection of the dark, sad Malvern Hills that Elgar loved and roamed and put into his incomparable music.

Buckinghamshire at its southern end is less than 15 miles from the Houses of Parliament in central London. Its beech woods near High Wycombe once supported the an-

cient craft of chair-bodging – making country chairs by turning the wood on a crude lathe. On a clear day you can see the Black Mountains in Wales from Coombe Hill, at 852 feet the highest point in the Chilterns. This was the setting chosen for Chequers, mediaeval house enlarged in Elizabethan times by the gaoler of Lady Jane Grey's sister Mary, which in 1917 became by gift the official weekend retreat for Britain's prime ministers. Only a few miles away is Hughenden, home of the great statesman Disraeli.

Oxfordshire, so very different from Cambridgeshire, has above all else Oxford – Oxenford – on the Thames, Matthew Arnold's 'sweet City with her dreaming spires'. Here has been England's oldest university since the early 12th century, the home of lost causes, which melted down its silver plate during the Civil War to fund the army of Charles I whose betrayal of the august role to which he had been called by birth had in the end to be redressed by his judicial, though violent, death. To explore this city walk, don't drive, for cars have tried for more than half a century to desecrate this ancient powerhouse of learning and panorama of architecture. Go down the High past

Queen's steps which once provided sanctuary, it is said, for malfeasant undergraduates, and look upon Magdalen Tower, at the top of which choir boys sing on May morning. Wander down St. Aldate's and listen as great Tom Tower on Christ Church College rings out the strokes of every hour on his mighty bell – Tom Tower was built by Wren, once Savilian Professor of Astronomy at Oxford. South-west of the city lies the famous Vale of White Horse, whose horse cut into the chalk on a hillside by ancient Celts might seem to herald the style of one of the periods of the great Pablo Picasso, 2,000 years later.

Northwards out of Oxford, less than ten miles, is Woodstock, where lived fair Rosamund, mistress of Henry II of England, the first Plantagenet. Nearby is Blenheim Palace, seat of Britain's foremost general, Marlborough, and behind it the village of Bladon in whose churchyard lies buried his descendant, Winston Churchill, surely the greatest of all Britain's many heroes. On to Witney, town of Cotswold stone, workshop for the famous blankets, flanked by the pretty River Windrush which a few miles to the west trickles softly past one of the most romantic settings in all England, the ruins of Minster Lovell, the home of Francis, Viscount Lovell, Richard III's loyal supporter.

Minster Lovell is next to Burford, the town on the steep hill with a motley collection of shops and trades on either side leading down to the river bridge, the gateway to Gloucestershire and thus to Cotswold country proper. Here, villages and towns lie sleepily amid long and pleasing stretches of crop and pasture land, often segmented by dry stone walling of vast lengths, grey stones piled one on another but with no mortar, enclosing famous Cotswold sheep, descendants of the mediaeval sheep that made English wool the most sought after in Europe and brought such wealth. Gloucestershire, famous for Tewkesbury with its huge abbey church and its streets of half-timbered houses, site of a desperate struggle between York and Lancaster in 1471; Cheltenham, a

The waters of the River Thames have provided power for this fine mill at Hambleden, Buckinghamshire since 1338, one of the few hundreds remaining of the thousands of watermills whose massive stones ground England's corn until the early part of this century.

John Radcliffe, an early 18th-century physician, left £40,000 for the building of this magnificent library, the Radcliffe Camera, Oxford, which is now a reading room attached to Oxford University's Bodleian Library. The architect, James Gibbs, probably based his design on drawings by Sir Christopher Wren for a round library at Trinity College, Cambridge.

DOMINVS · CVSTODIAT · INTROITVM · TVVM · ET · EXITVM · TVVM

spa with mineral springs favoured by Regency bucks whose planned streets of Georgian houses are an architectural landmark; and Gloucester itself with its ancient cathedral which once was threatened with demolition to make way for a multi-storey carpark.

At Gloucestershire's western edge is the Forest of Dean, once a centre of iron-making from nearby ores smelted with its charcoal. Follow the glorious Wye valley into the lush, tightly knit fields of the county of Hereford and Worcester, once two separate counties. Some of the fields are on flat ground, more perched precariously on hillsides, fields that produce apples, pears, hops and pasture for the famous Herefordshire cattle. Hereford city's streets with their amazingly mixed periods of houses jostle the ancient cathedral of 11th-century origins, with its chained library and the *Mappa Mundi*, a 13th-century map of the world.

In the east of the county is historic Worcestershire – apple and plum orchards in the Vale of Evesham, carpet making in Kidderminster, brine springs at Droitwich, and battle sites famous in British history, notably at Evesham in 1265 where fell the 'Good Earl' Simon de Montfort, founder of Parliament, and at Worcester in 1651, 'the crowning mercy' as Cromwell who won it coined the phrase. In Norman-built Worcester Cathedral, over 400 feet long, centre of the world renowned Three Choirs Festival, much-maligned King John is buried, he who rightly declined to keep promises extracted in Magna Carta because he knew they gave not liberty to the people but licence to the barons.

Shakespeare's River Avon runs through the Vale of Evesham from

The River Windrush flows past lawns and under small bridges alongside the main street of this charming Cotswold village in Gloucestershire, Bourton-on-the-Water (*left*) which is entirely built of amber-coloured local stone.

The birthplace of Sir Winston Churchill, Blenheim Palace, Oxford (*below*) was given to the first Duke of Marlborough in Queen Anne's reign as a reward for his military victories. This magnificent baroque-style palace, designed by Sir John Vanbrugh, was completed in 1722 and contains work by some of the greatest artists and craftsmen of the day.

Compton Winyates, Warwickshire, built around the turn of the 15th century, is one of the finest Tudor mansions in England. Its spiralling chimneys, pinkish brickwork, stone coins and mullions and fantastically clipped yew trees give this spot near Banbury its particular Tudor charm.

The Royal Shakespeare Theatre was built in 1932 to replace the one destroyed by fire in 1926. Swans glide gracefully past the new theatre on the river at Stratford-upon-Avon, the birthplace of Shakespeare, the world's greatest dramatist.

Warwickshire. On its banks is Stratford, where in 1564 the greatest poet and playwright of all time was born. Stratford is understandably full of Shakespeare: Ann Hathaway's preserved cottage, a fine 1930s theatre holding a season every year with the world's great actors, and the Bard's own birthplace. There is much more to Warwickshire, though, for it has

Kenilworth Castle and the new Coventry Cathedral built by Basil Spence, which stands guard over the ruins of the old one destroyed by German bombs in 1941. Warwick town has the mediaeval castle dominated by the 133-foot tall Caesar's Tower, Royal Leamington Spa, which Queen Victoria so named after a memorable visit to enjoy its waters. North of Warwickshire is the county of West Midlands of which Birmingham, second city of England, is the centre. It is vast, sprawling, in many respects shapeless and monolithic,

and yet magnificent because of its inner strength and what it represents – the hub of British industry and mechanical enterprise.

Northamptonshire suffers from the reputation of always being on the way to somewhere else, but it is worth lingering among its villages and towns built of native county stone of many kinds, such as Weldon and Colly Weston, and stopping to see the churches of Brixworth and Earl's Barton, both begun in the 8th century and among the oldest surviving Saxon buildings in the country.

The West Country – once the kingdom of Wessex – was the land of the West Saxons, who under Cerdic and Ceawlin, pushed the British peoples in the 5th and 6th centuries into the fastnesses of their kinfolk's lands in Wales and the North West, and laid the foundations of a kingdom that was to stretch from Devon to the Kent border, from London to Bristol. Today Wessex, the name revived through the novels of Dorset-born Thomas Hardy, embraces Somerset, Avon, Wiltshire, Hampshire, Dorset, Devon and the ancient Celtic kingdom of Cornwall, or Kernow, that was never part of old Wessex. It is mainly hilly countryside – in parts of Devon almost mountainous, has more than its fair share of rain, it seems, and draws more visitors to its coast resorts, its cities and its charming and picturesque villages than perhaps any other English region.

Avon is enviably proud of Bristol, one of England's oldest port towns, from which the Cabots, father and son, set sail in 1497 and discovered Newfoundland. Bristol – its university; its Clifton Suspension Bridge across the superb Avon Gorge, masterpiece of design by Isambard Kingdom Brunel, Britain's 19th-century Leonardo, but completed in his memory by his colleagues; its two cathedrals, Anglican and Roman

The majestic sweep of the Royal Crescent was the apex of the reconstruction of Bath as a fashionable spa during the Georgian period. There remains a Regency air about Bath, in spite of modernisation, and many of the views across the town have scarcely changed since John Wood masterminded the rebuilding.

Catholic. Another fine city dominates the county of Avon: Bath, popular among Romans for its hot chalybeate springs (they called it *Aquae Sulis*), and among Georgians, too, who built its famous Pump Room and raised many of its splendid streets and crescents of houses within a stone's throw of its great Perpendicular abbey.

Twenty-one miles to the southwest of Bath lies Wells in Somerset, a tiny city like Ely, and with a huge cathedral in this valley site, one with a west front almost unequalled in Europe for its decorative treatment. The Somerset countryside is full of contrast; flat, marshy land between Wells and Taunton, at Athelney where great Alfred lay in hiding waiting his chance later to smash the Danes and at Glastonbury where early Christians worshipped and some believe King Arthur was laid to rest; the lead-bearing Mendips and the glorious Quantocks. At Cheddar is a fantastic gorge of limestone, several hundred feet deep, at the bottom of which you can walk or drive to the world-famous caves.

Soaring to 404 feet, the graceful spire of Salisbury Cathedral, Wiltshire (*right*) is the highest in England. It was added in the 14th century following the completion of the main building which remarkably took only 60 years to plan and build from its conception in 1220.

This 14th-century tower on Glastonbury Tor in Somerset (*below*) marks the site of an ancient chapel, under which, it is said, was buried the cup used at the Last Supper.

To the east of Avon and Somerset the land rises steeply into Wiltshire, where the vast and seemingly borderless fields and downs of Salisbury Plain stretch from Devizes to the mediaeval city of Salisbury that was founded in the 1220s when the earlier cathedral of Old Sarum, about a mile north on the hillside, was abandoned because of running aggravation between clerics and the inhabitants of Old Sarum Castle. The cathedral at Salisbury, an Early English architectural whole, with its spire over 400 feet tall, was immortalized by Constable. Wiltshire abounds in barrows long and round (prehistoric burial mounds), stone circles (notably Avebury) and of course Stonehenge. Wiltshire's fields produce fine crops and sheep and cattle, on which the villages of brick and flint and timber have long thrived. In the north is Swindon – Sweyn's dune – a strange amalgam of residential Old Town on the hill, railway town inspired by Brunel with houses of limestone graded according to rank in the railway service, and modern overspill settlement for 'emigrant' Londoners. Swindon's new Princess Margaret Hospital is one of the few modern structures to which the word graceful can properly be accorded.

Drop down from Swindon past Liddington Hill where some now believe the last stand of the Britons against the Saxons, the battle of Mount Badon, was fought at the end of the 5th century. Then travel on

into Hampshire to Winchester, capital of Alfred, the only English king ever to earn the title The Great, one richly deserved. He made Wessex the sovereign power of England. Transformed by his tutor Swithun, Bishop of Winchester, from an unlettered scion of the royal house of Ecgbert into a leading intellectual light, Viking-breaker and warship-builder, Alfred set in train his tremendous educational programme carried forward by scholars picked from Wales and Ireland that catapulted England into the mainstream of European scholarship. And on the ground of Swithun's church rose the longest mediaeval church in England, Winchester cathedral. Thirteen miles south is the Anglo-Saxon port town Southampton, some of its environs occupied since the Stone Age, used by Roman, Saxon and Norman, and developed into the major passenger port of Britain today. Navy days at Portsmouth dockyard, 20 miles away, give one the chance to see the *Victory*, flagship and hearse of Nelson, the greatest admiral in the history of the world. Retrace your steps westwards through the dense and mysterious New Forest, exclusive hunting ground for William the Conqueror, with dire penalties for trespassing, in which his able but slandered son and heir,

These whitewashed cottages on a hillside at North Bovey, Devon (*right*) have a wonderful view across Dartmoor from their windows. They are stoutly built of cob, a mixture of earth and straw, and stone.

Stonehenge, on Salisbury Plain in Wiltshire (*left*) was constructed nearly 4,000 years ago. The positioning of the double circle of huge stones is thought to have been of religious and astronomical significance.

William Rufus, met his death from an arrow through the heart.

Head west to Dorset, renowned for its quarries at Portland and Purbeck whose stone decorates or forms the structure for buildings throughout the land. Kings loved the castle at Corfe, especially John who adorned this tough, military group of buildings with his palace suite, the 'Gloriette', the whole sadly wrecked in over-zealous dismantling after the Civil War. Almost all Dorset's coastline is of outstanding natural beauty, designated so, and no wonder. For wonderful scenery it is worth taking the coast road from Weymouth, passing Chesil Beach to Lyme Regis.

Devon, the second largest county before the boundary changing in 1974, is suspended as it were round two upland expanses, Exmoor in the north and Dartmoor in the south. Exmoor, wild, heather-dressed, scoured by ponies, sheep and deer in search of sustenance, is the backdrop for many coastal resorts and sea villages, notably Ilfracombe and Lynmouth. Dartmoor, in contrast, is grey, sinister, misty, primordial, littered with clumps of volcanic detritus, the famous tors dramatically evoked in Conan Doyle's *The Hound of the Baskervilles*, with here and there oases of life such as the small towns of Widecombe and Chagford and Bovey Tracey. Devon's county town is Exeter, with the finest Decorated Gothic cathedral in the country and one of the earliest Norman stone gate-towers, built soon after the Hastings confrontation. On the south coast is the naval port of Plymouth which has set the scene for many famous expeditions.

Cross the River Tamar westwards, by road or over Brunel's wonderful Saltash Bridge by train, from Plymouth, and when you get to the other side, it is almost like not being in England any more. This is Cornwall, ancient Celtic kingdom, land of tin mines and smugglers' coves, tiny seaside towns and villages with narrow, winding streets and clustered houses, tidy inland market towns with picturesque names like Lostwithiel, Bodmin, Camelford, Perranporth, fishing port towns like Falmouth and Penzance, and the cathedral city of Truro, whose grammar school was founded by Edward VI in 1549.

Cornwall's ancient traditions are kept alive by the National Party, Mebyon Kernow, which fields candidates at local elections and wins seats.

Rugged broken cliffs and granite rocks jut cruelly into the sea at Land's End, Cornwall (*right*), England's farthest western point. On a calm day it seems quite peaceful, but this part of the Cornish coast is treacherous and has earned itself the name of the Sailor's Graveyard.

Village life centres around the comings and goings of boats in the harbour at Mevagissey, Cornwall. In days gone by the villagers used to make a living fishing for pilchards and smuggling. The latter is now a thing of the past, replaced with a thriving tourist trade.

England

The Midlands and the North West

This 16th-century timbered gatehouse (*far right*) is at the entrance to Stokesay Castle, a medieval fortification with a castle wall and moat and very fine Great Hall. The tower has a 17th-century half-timbered gallery round the top.

Chester's brightly coloured clock adorns medieval Eastgate (*below*), one of the main gates through the city wall and now a main thoroughfare. The clock, installed in 1897, commemorates Queen Victoria's Diamond Jubilee.

One of the loveliest drives in England is along the A49 from Hereford through the county of Salop, one of the border counties between England and Wales. Here you can visit ancient Ludlow town, perched on a steep hill, with a famous castle on the top that overlooks the Teme river valley below. To the north are the Clee Hills, Brown Clee, nearly 1,800 feet high, and her sister peak, Titterstone Clee. On, then, through more of the Shropshire Hills to the county town of Shrewsbury, also on high ground and plunging low into the Severn, where one July day in 1403 great Harry Hotspur fought and lost a battle with Henry Bolingbroke (Henry IV). Salop is mostly farming country, yet was not overlooked in the Industrial Revolution, for at Coalbrookdale, ironstone quarries fed early ironworks, yielding the raw material for the first iron bridge in the world, erected here in 1779.

Salop flanks the western side of Staffordshire and, like Surrey, is a county neglected by travel writers, who in this case are perhaps blinded by the grey, drab, powdery basin of the Trent in and around Stoke where lie the world-famous Potteries (now transformed after the Clean Air Act) and the blacker, grittier areas of ironstone and coal like Cannock Chase (once a famous hunting ground and still a local beauty spot), a bracken-covered ridge bulging with minerals. Staffordshire has its own university at Keele, a post-war foundation distinguished for the originality of its studies. The city of Lichfield was the birthplace of Samuel Johnson and home of the cathedral whose three spires of the 13th-14th centuries are known as the Ladies of the Vale, and whose treasures include an 8th-century illuminated Book of Gospels that has been there for over a thousand years.

Across the north-west border of Staffordshire you come to low-lying fertile Cheshire, studded with mediaeval and post-mediaeval houses. It was once a county palatine – a county whose king-appointed ruler had special powers to deal with the dangerous local conditions – bordering as it did on fierce, wild, independent Wales. Its capital was, and still is, Chester, old Roman legionary fortress of *Deva*, later a mediaeval city with a castle and enclosing walls and a monastery church that in 1541 became a cathedral. Cheshire provides the get-away-from-it-all countryside and the attractive little coast towns in the Wirral peninsula where hard-working Lancashire

Little Moreton Hall, Cheshire, is a glorious example of the Tudor delight in carving and ornamentation. The gable ends, the doors and the corner posts are all elaborately carved; inside the fireplaces are decorated with heraldic carvings and the long gallery retains the original panelling. The tall, moated house has scarcely changed since it was completed in 1580.

This lovely village of Sawrey in Cumbria — where Beatrix Potter, of Peter Rabbit fame, wrote most of her books at Hill Top Farm — is in the Southern Lakes, an area where Herdwicks, the Lakeland's own breed of sheep, are raised.

business men can relax. Two major rivers form part of Cheshire's boundaries, the Dee on the west and the great Mersey in the north.

The metropolitan county of Merseyside has of course become a famous name because of the fabulous four – John, Paul, George and Ringo – who transformed British, indeed global, pop music, and first made their names in their native Liverpool.

But Liverpool has for long been one of the sights of Merseyside. Recognized for its potential as a port for Ireland by King John who granted it a charter in 1207, this splendid city came into its own with the development of the Lancashire cotton industry in the last century, becoming second port in England to London. Its international predominance is signalled by the marvellous skyline

eye-catcher, the Royal Liver Building of 1911, twin-towered and nearly 300 feet tall, on the water's edge. Liverpool has two great cathedrals; the Anglican cathedral, completed in 1979 and now the biggest church in Britain, and the remarkable Roman Catholic Cathedral of Christ the King built by Sir Frederick Gibberd upon a fantastic brickwork crypt of Sir Edwin Lutyens. The medical

faculty of its university is among the foremost in the western world.

Liverpool faces its sister port and shipyard town, Birkenhead, on the other bank of the Mersey at the northern tip of the Wirral, and you can travel from one to the other by ferry, by rail through one Mersey tunnel and by road through another, the Queensway. Birkenhead had the first trams in Europe, regrettably replaced by less reliable omnibuses.

North of Merseyside is Lancashire, beautiful to its millions of proud natives, whether they live in little stone cottages in those patches of unspoilt countryside scattered amid the great industrial spread, or in narrow streets or tower blocks at Salford or Blackburn, Wigan or Rochdale, or great Manchester itself. 'Foreigners', and that includes Yorkshiremen!, may not all agree, but don't be put off travelling through this amazing county, full of contrasts: flat land covered with industrial history, the heights of the Pennine Chain to the east, mountains spilling over from Cumbria in the north, and on the west the sea resorts, Blackpool, Morecambe and Southport, meccas of ice cream, Gracie

For years the workers from the northern factories have spent their holidays at Blackpool, with its many amusements and miles of golden sands. At night, a multitude of lights illuminate Blackpool Tower and the promenade.

Fields and flower festivals. Consider what Lancashire has given the world – from Rochdale the Pioneers who in 1844 founded the first Cooperative Society in England, from Wigan pain-relieving ball-joint operations for osteo-arthritis of the hip, from Blackburn James Hargreaves, inventor of the spinning jenny, from Warrington the first rate-supported free public library. And think of Manchester itself, where Rutherford, the greatest experimental physicist of all time, split the atom in 1919, and where Cobden and Bright founded the Anti-Corn Law League in 1838 heralding the concept of free trade. Manchester has numerous fine buildings such as the Free Trade Hall, the 15th-century church that became a cathedral in 1847, Liverpool Road Station, the first passenger station in the world, Barton Arcade with its glass roof and the Shambles, post-mediaeval aggregate of houses and inns preserved amid the new Arndale development.

would follow Roman and not Irish Christianity, and the tremendously popular sea resort of Scarborough, with its homely hotels and boarding houses that have accommodated holiday-makers since Victorian days, and its castle built by Henry II and besieged time and again, even shelled in the First World War.

On the edge of the North Riding are the beginnings of the breathtaking Yorkshire Dales, cut through by rivers like the Swale, the Nidd, the Ure and the Wharfe. Nidderdale and Wharfedale lead into the West Riding, cross it and blend into the Pennines where the rivers rise.

The West Riding, largest of the three ridings, sharply contrasting in its highland scenery with its massive

industrial sprawl lower down, has a veritable roll-call of British industrial history. Factories and mineshafts may not seem places of beauty and yet the sheer size, the expanse, the energy of the industrial centres in this vibrant part of Yorkshire excite warmth and wonder. Leeds, wool centre since the Middle Ages, has a university and medical school of international standing. Bradford, where the first spinning factory was opened in 1798 and where Delius was born in 1863, has one of the most celebrated grammar schools in England. Huddersfield, a centre of the textile industry, has roots going back to Anglo-Saxon times; and Barnsley is sited on rich coalfields. Wakefield, cathedral city and once capital of the

The rich vein of Yorkshire agriculture is revealed in this scene of haymaking in Swaledale, one of the four great dales which run from the bleak and craggy Yorkshire moors to the gentler Vale of York.

In the Middle Ages Bootham Bar, this great stone gateway (*right*) guarded the city of York against attacks from the north. Behind it rise the magnificent towers of York Minster, the largest Gothic church in England.

West Riding, was the site of a great defeat of the Yorkists in 1460 under Richard Plantagenet, Duke of York, who sallied forth from his castle at nearby Sandal and never returned. Sandal has recently been the subject of the most exciting castle excavations of this century and is now open

46

The ruins of Bolton Abbey stand in splendid isolation on a bend of the River Wharfe, five miles from Ilkley. Founded as an Augustinian priory in 1150, the abbey was largely destroyed during the Dissolution of the Monasteries in the 16th century, although the nave still stands and is used occasionally for services.

Castle Howard, near Malton, Yorkshire (*top*) is among the largest and most spectacular houses in England; like its contemporary Blenheim Palace, it was designed by Sir John Vanbrugh.

The greatest days of Whitby, Yorkshire (*above*) were in the 18th century, when it was a major whaling port, but the town still gains its livelihood from fishing the North Sea.

for all to see. Pontefract's mediaeval castle, now a ruin, was once the grandest in the north of England. There is something inspiring about this great industrial basin: it exudes confidence, and in times of recession it infuses one with the feeling that, fundamentally, things are all right with British industry.

At the point where the Ridings meet is the Ainsty of York, a six-square-mile enclave consisting of the city of York and some surrounding land. York has figured large throughout English history. Once a Celtic settlement it then became a Roman military capital of the north of occupied Britain, where Flavius Valerius Aurelius Constantinus was proclaimed Emperor Constantine I in 306 by his troops. An archbishopric was established as long ago as 732 and York Minster, a massive cathedral of overpowering beauty, was begun in the 1220s. Today, it is one of the greatest tourist centres, with its mediaeval city wall intact for much of its original length, its Clifford's Tower quatre-foil plan great tower castle on a high mound, its national railway museum, its picturesque streets with names like Fossgate, Monkgate, Micklegate, Gillygate, and its remarkable covered series of reconstructed Georgian and Victorian streets.

The Lake District and Northumberland

North of the North Yorkshire Moors is the county of Durham and the new county of Cleveland which has Middlesborough as its county town. County Durham was an ancient county palatine, whose prince-bishops exercised almost regal authority for centuries. The coalfields are among the richest in Britain. For great distances the countryside is bleak and grey, darkened by industrial smoke and haze, but beautiful nonetheless. Take the train from Darlington, one of the very first railway stations in the world, and prepare for the approach to the bridge over the River Wear at Durham city. Suddenly as you begin to cross the river valley you see to your right the massive twin towers of the cathedral's west front and, soaring

above them and a little behind, the great central tower over the crossing. It is an astonishing sight, this edifice of three fingers reaching upwards. Here are buried the remains of the first historian of the English people, the Venerable Bede, the devout and scholarly monk who worked and died at the monastery at Jarrow. He would surely have welcomed the creation of the University of Durham, England's third, in 1832 – now a leading centre for classical studies.

The west part of the county becomes mountainous as it rises into the Pennines, and there you cross into Cumbria, to a part of the county once known as Westmorland, yet another ancient county – this one founded in 1100 – curtly wiped off the face of the administrative map of England in

1974, but still very much a district with a character of its own. Its neighbouring county of Cumberland to the north also disappeared to make the one much larger county of Cumbria. The old county of Westmorland is part of the Lake District. It is sometimes called Wordsworth country, for though the great poet was born at Cockermouth in neighbouring Cumberland, he retired to Grasmere and spent the last half-century or so of his life there, writing, talking, walking and enjoying the company of family and friends, be-

Built on an outcrop of sandstone almost surrounded by the River Wear, the great Norman Romanesque cathedral of Durham is not only a house of God: Durham Castle forms its northern wing and the Norman kings gave the bishops of Durham military powers.

Seen past bare-branched silver birches, the little town of Keswick (*left*), where copper and graphite used to be mined, seems protected, almost hidden, by the slopes of Skiddaw. This gentle mountain is a surprising 3,000 feet above sea level and is the fourth highest of the Lakeland fells.

The most famous view in all Cumbria is Derwentwater (*below*). Everything is there: the wooded islands on the lake, the fertile shore and the majestic fells beyond.

coming Poet Laureate in succession to Robert Southey who also lived and died in Westmorland.

Wordsworth and his friends and visitors made the Lake District famous. They opened it up, as it were, to people from all walks of life, who went there for holidays, walking tours, to paint, to write, to practise crafts, to compose, and to learn how to climb mountains and to keep fit through arduous outdoor exercises and camping out in bad weather. Other great men retired to live there, like John Ruskin, slowly and sadly going out of his mind at Brantwood, his home by Coniston Water.

What is there about the Lake District that inspires creative people, draws them to its landscapes? It is perhaps the seemingly endless procession of mountains and lakes,

streams and waterfalls, dales and rocks, which overwhelm the imagination. Of its 15 great lakes, Windermere is over ten miles long, Ullswater is more than seven miles long, its southern reaches probably the most beautiful of all Lakeland scenery, and Coniston Water, five miles long, is the most placid of all lakes, and yet, because of this, is sadly the graveyard of Donald Campbell after his attempt to break the world water speed record in 1967.

Lakes are but one kind of natural glory. There are more than 100 mountains in the Lake District over 2,000 feet. They are known as fells in Cumbria and the highest, Scafell Pike, is 3,206 feet high. This majestic mountain, the tallest in England, glowers over Derwentwater. Helvellyn, over 3,100 feet, dominates

This great ring of ancient stones in Cumbria is known variously as Castlerigg or Keswick Carles. The tallest stones stand in line with the summits of Hellvellyn (in the background) and Skiddaw, and the ring, like Stonehenge, probably had astronomical significance.

abbot; Dryburgh, raised by Premonstratensians in the 1140s, where Walter Scott is buried; and Kelso, erected on the banks of the Tweed in the 1120s for the Tironensians. Jedburgh, the finest of the four, is in the old royal burgh where in October 1566 Mary, Queen of Scots dallied with Bothwell in Queen Mary's House while her husband Darnley lodged a few doors away.

Follow the Tweed eastwards, skirted for most of the way by the A698, to the border town of Berwick upon Tweed. This key position on the river mouth, held alternately by Scots and English throughout the Middle Ages until the end of the 15th century when it became English for good, was for long treated as a separate entity, not within a county, until the 1880s when it was absorbed into Northumberland.

The Great North Road comes out of England through Berwick and skirts the eastern coast, swings round and ends with a triumphant flourish at the approaches to Princes Street in glorious Edinburgh. On or beside its route, there are crucial historical sites like Dunbar, scene of Cromwell's great victory of 1650 over those Scots unwise enough to champion the cause of Charles I's heir, Prince Charles; Tantallon Castle, stronghold of the mighty Douglas family, perched upon the rocky coast overlooking the Firth of Forth, besieged unsuccessfully by James V in 1526 with troops marching against it chanting 'Ding Doun, Tantalloun!'; and Prestonpans where in 1745 Bonnie Prince Charlie thrashed the London government's troops sent to resist the prince's struggle to win the throne for his father, Prince James Edward.

The last meandering miles of the River Tweed, before it enters the North Sea at Berwick, mark the boundary between Scotland and England. Farther upstream, where the boundary rises to the crest of the Cheviot Hills, the Tweed flows through its own deep and luxuriant Scottish valley. It is a salmon river producing fish in such abundance that local servants used to complain at being fed salmon daily!

Scotland

From the Clyde to the Forth

If the Southern Uplands of Scotland may seem here and there wild and poor, with huge, dramatic landscapes bereft of human habitation, the great Midland Valley from the Firth of Clyde to the Firth of Forth, with its tentacles up the north-eastern coastal plains, is Scotland's fount of wealth. It has been so from the earliest times, since Pict and Scot, Angle and Norman realized and coveted the farming potential of its fertile ground. And when Britain moved into its industrial glory, this Midland Valley, dominated then as now by three great towns – points of a triangle each in a different county – Glasgow, Stirling and Edinburgh, was to prove as fruitful a ground as anywhere in Britain, with abundant coalfields to power a profusion of industries while the business of farming went on without cease. Thus it is today.

Glasgow in Strathclyde is the third city of Britain, with almost a million people. It was once a basin for shipbuilding, second to none in quality and tonnage, and still among the foremost industrial centres of the world. Its roots reach far back into Scotland's history, to St. Kentigern (also called St. Mungo) believed to

This elegant road bridge, at 8,244 feet one of the longest suspension bridges in the world, spans the Firth of Forth, linking Edinburgh with Dundee and the North Sea oil port of Aberdeen. The bridge, opened by the Queen in 1964, makes a fine contrast with the cantilevered Forth Rail Bridge running parallel, which was built in the 1880s.

A statue of Sir Walter Scott, the celebrated 19th-century poet and novelist, tops a fluted Doric column in Glasgow's spacious and elegant George Square, which was laid out in 1768 and is still a fashionable centre of the city.

have been the friend of St. Columba who persuaded him to found Glasgow's church that was to become St. Mungo's Cathedral in the 12th and 13th centuries. Scotland cannot be understood without a tour of Glasgow, city with two universities (one, Glasgow, founded in 1451, the second university in Scotland, and Strathclyde, created in 1966 from the old Andersonian Technical College – Livingstone was one of many of its students). Glasgow was disastrously burned in a great fire in 1677 then was splendidly rebuilt in Scottish stone by Scottish craftsmen, provoking Daniel Defoe in 1707, the year of the Act of Union, to describe it as

one of the 'cleanliest and ... most beautiful cities in Great Britain ...' Worth seeing also are the Broomielaw Bridge of the 1760s and the Forth-Clyde Canal linking the west to the east.

Another link between west and east is the famous Antonine Wall, a long earthwork ditch and rampart stretching from Old Kilpatrick on the Clyde to Bo'ness on the Forth. This was built in the time of Emperor Antoninus Pius, in the 140s A.D. It has remains of earthwork and stonework in its forts along its 37 miles: Rough Castle, near Bonnybridge, a square-plan one-acre fort surrounded by narrow double ditching, and Bar

Hill, near Kilsyth, a three-acre fort excavated 80 years ago.

Just south of the wall, twelve miles from Glasgow, is Cumbernauld new town, rightly winner of world acclaim for its layout. Go north again and you will travel through countryside that witnessed some of the great struggles for independence in the days of England's arrogant Edward I, which culminated in the magnificent victory of Robert Bruce over Edward's son at Bannockburn in 1314, under the shadow of the huge basalt rock mound of Stirling which rises some 250 feet from the ground below. On it stands the great castle, begun in the 12th century, part of its structure overhanging the sheer cliff face. The marvellous Great Hall of James III is reckoned the finest 15th-century Renaissance building in Britain.

From the battlements of Stirling you can see, 20 miles away, the two vast bridges across the Forth, the lace-like cantilevered 19th-century rail bridge and the new suspension road bridge. On fine days, the 270-foot basalt rock mound supporting Edinburgh's massive castle complex

The highlight of every Edinburgh Festival is the Military Tattoo which takes place nightly in Edinburgh Castle – the great stone fortress, built on a massive rock of basalt, which dominates the city. Although the site has been fortified since the Iron Age, almost all the early buildings have been destroyed by wars during its turbulent history, and the present castle buildings only date back to the 16th century.

Princes Street, justly called one of the most beautiful streets anywhere, borders Edinburgh's handsome Georgian New Town on one side, and on the other gives a clear view past the Scott Memorial to the tall tenements of the Old Town and the great castle.

is visible, some 37 miles away. It was begun in Malcolm III's time in the 11th century but was almost all rebuilt in later times. This complex has been more than a fortress; it has been a royal treasury, an arsenal, an archive of national records, and a refuge for Scotland's kings during their tender years, when they were threatened by greedy, ambitious nobles.

Edinburgh, capital of Scotland since the end of the Middle Ages, is often described as the 'Athens of the North', and is the centre for the world-famous Edinburgh Festival. It possesses two universities, the first opened in 1583 (at that time it was Scotland's fourth university when England still had only two), the second, Heriot-Watt, opened in 1966, and its own Parliament House, now used as law courts. Edinburgh is perhaps most celebrated of all for its 18th-century New Town – whose principal feature, Princes Street, is one of the loveliest anywhere – a town built as an extension of the old upon reclaimed marshy ground at Nor'Loch under the shadow of the castle rock, marvellously laid out in an ordered grid of fine streets, squares, crescents and gardens, with houses designed by the best British architects, notably William Adam and his sons, including the celebrated Robert Adam.

The Palace of Holyroodhouse, at the east end of Edinburgh's Royal Mile, was given its present imposing form by Charles II in 1676. There had been a royal residence at Holyrood since 1128, when David I founded an abbey there with a guesthouse for Scotland's kings. Later, when Edinburgh became the capital city, James IV started work on the palace buildings.

Scotland

The North East

The Midland Valley in Central Scotland pushes its farming plains into the east, to Perth, once capital of Scotland, and to nearby Scone, an even older Pictish capital. In Fife, the county that was once a kingdom, lies Dumfermline Abbey where the great Robert Bruce lies buried. To the east is Kirkcaldy, sometimes called the 'lang toon' because its main street is nearly four miles long. And just outside is Ravenscraig Castle, begun by James II in 1460, the first castle in all Britain to be specially designed for artillery. On the north-east coast of the county is St. Andrews, with its ruined 12th-century cathedral, its university, Scotland's oldest, founded in 1411, and its castle which in 1547 was successfully entered by besiegers tunnelling through the living rock on which it stands. Over the Firth of Tay is Dundee, centre of the jute industry, a university town and home of a provincial newspaper chain where many of the best journalists of the English-speaking world have learned their craft. A fine new road bridge complements the railway bridge beside, replacement for one

Throwing the hammer at the Braemar Highland Games. The weighted hammer is swung round on a flexible handle before being let go. Games, or Gatherings, are held at Highland centres throughout the summer, with competitions in dancing reels, playing the bagpipes, tossing the caber and putting the weight.

As the sun goes down behind the graceful cone of Schiehallion, 'fairy hill of the Caledonians', it is reflected in the waters of Loch Tummel. At 3,547 feet above sea level, Schiehallion in Tayside dominates Glen Tummel, which lies beyond the loch, and the lonely wastes of Rannoch Moor.

Castle Campbell, Dollar, stands in proud isolation amid breathtaking wooded scenery, not far from the Firth of Forth. The First Earl of Argyll, head of the Clan Campbell, built the tower house in the 15th century, and his descendants added the lesser buildings over the next two centuries.

designed in the 1870s by Sir Thomas Bouch so poorly that, tragically, it collapsed in a storm just after Christmas in 1879, carrying with it a trainload of 75 victims to a watery grave.

Dundee is the beginning of Tayside, formerly Angus and before that Forfarshire, county of the Braes of Angus, part of the vast Grampian range that spreads across Scotland from east to west in a huge arc. Thirty miles north-east of Dundee is Brechin, a city with a bishopric going back to the 1100s and a cathedral of the 13th century.

North-east of Tayside is Grampian which embraces the historic counties of Aberdeenshire, Kincardineshire, Banffshire and most of Morayshire. To the west lie the eerie and desolate Cairngorms, crisp with snow in cold winter for ski-slopes, and seeming to hide the sun from the lower lying land where Aberdeen Angus cattle graze. On the coast is the ancient granite city of Aberdeen, hewn stone block by stone block from the ground on which it spreads. Its university, the third in Scotland and founded in 1495, has one building, Marischal College, 'a poem in stone', said to be the second largest granite building in the world. Aberdeen, rich since the Middle Ages from fishing, ship construction and commerce, became a boom town in the 1960s as North Sea oil began to be exploited and rigs and their crews needed the services of a modern port city.

In the hills north-west of Aberdeen, near Inverurie, a Roman legionary camp was found at Durno in 1975, which its discoverers claim proves that the great battle of Mons Graupius between Romans and

The grey coastal city of St. Andrews, Fife, renowned as an international centre for the game of golf, has the oldest university in Britain (established in 1411) and was once Scotland's ecclesiastical capital. Its cathedral and priory, founded in 1160, flourished until 1559 when a mob, inflamed by the preaching of the fiery Protestant John Knox, set about 'casting it doon'. In 1649 Cromwell encouraged its use as a quarry for building stone, and soon its ruin was complete.

Caledonians, of A.D. 84, was fought nearby, a battle described by the Romans as a resounding victory, but which seems now to have been a strategic reverse for them.

North-west is Elgin, where once the most beautiful of all Scottish cathedrals, Elgin, is now a ruin. Begun in the 1220s, burned in 1390 in a raid by the Wolf of Badenoch, nickname for Alexander Stewart, youngest brother of Robert III, it was restored but despoiled again. Elgin is

on the road to Inverness, the A98, and as you push on towards the capital of the Highlands, some way south of your route are thousands more square miles of mountain land, fissured by the great sport-fishing rivers, the Spey and the Findhorn. The countryside by the road grows less pretty and seems perpetually under clouds, heralding the flatter, here-and-there wooded, moorland which brings you to Culloden, where died the last hopes of the Jacobites who

sought to place a Scottish king upon the throne, his by right of descent but barred by the Act of Settlement because of his Roman Catholic religion.

It was more than the Jacobite cause that fell at Culloden, that day in 1746: it was the ancient Scottish nation. Something of that finality can be felt if you stop to reflect upon the battlefield, clothed in an air of depression that hangs over the whole area.

Dunnotar Castle near Stonehaven looks impregnable. It stands on a rocky promontory 160 feet above the turbulent North Sea, with no more than a narrow isthmus connecting it with the mainland. Despite its strong position it has been taken several times, notably by William Wallace in 1296 and by Cromwell's Roundheads after an eight-month siege in 1652. It was dismantled after the Jacobite rising of 1715 and fell into ruin, but recently some of the rooms have been restored.

The home of the ancient Lyon family and the earls of Strathmore, whose most famous descendant is Queen Elizabeth the Queen Mother, Glamis Castle near Forfar in Tayside is a splendid example of the Scottish baronial style. The great tower was built in the 15th century and the decorative turrets, corbels and residential wings, reminiscent of a French château, were added in the late 17th century. Inside there are some fine Renaissance plaster ceilings.

The Highlands and Islands

St. Columba settled on the island of Iona in A.D. 563 when he came from Ireland to spread Christianity among the Scots. His foundation was attacked so often by the Norsemen that nothing remains of it except his own cell, and the stone slab he is said to have slept on; but Iona came to be regarded as so holy a place that nearly all Scotland's early kings, including Macbeth, were buried there. The early part of this century saw the restoration of much of this beautiful 13th-century Benedictine abbey.

Stirling in Central Scotland is the bridge between the Midland Valley and the northern half of Scotland. It dominates all the main routes to north and south, as well as to east and west. It is the gateway to the Highlands, that part of Scotland north, roughly, of a line from Dumbarton Castle in the west to Dunnottar Castle in the east, almost a separate land with its vast, mountainous, deserted, primitive scenery, inter-spersed with inland and sea lochs, tumbling rivers and waterfalls, clean, bright towns, monuments of stone hundreds – sometimes thousands – of years old, and on the western side flanked by numerous islands.

The Highlands formed the terri-tory that became the first kingdom of Scotia when bold Kenneth Mac-Alpin – ancestor of all the Scottish kings – welded together Pict and Scot in the early 9th century, set up his

Highland cattle, with their branching horns and long shaggy reddish coats, are indigenous to the West Highlands. These pastures are on the banks on Loch Linnhe, a long sea loch which has carved a deep channel from the Firth of Lorne and the Sound of Mull to the Great Glen, which almost divides Scotland in half.

capital at Perth and advanced towards the Forth-Clyde line to bring Strathclyde and the Lothians into his orbit. Steeped in history and prehistory and largely rendered desolate by the infamous Clearances of the 18th and 19th centuries, the Highlands are still Roman Catholic in many parts, still Gaelic speaking here and there, and still clannish. Grim, mediaeval fortresses like Duart in Mull, Dunollie near Oban and Dunvegan on Skye are still owned by the clans which in the turbulent Middle Ages used them to resist attempts of the Scottish Crown to bring the Highlands to heel.

From Stirling head through the gentle, wooded Trossachs and wind your way along fine roads into the north of Strathclyde, once Argyll-shire, past tall mountains and deep inland lochs like Loch Awe and Loch Etive, and on to Oban, delightful seaport and holiday town, quite unspoiled, with the two ancient castles, Dunollie and Dunstaffnage, nearby. Dunollie was once the seat of the great Somerled, Lord of Argyll and founder of the MacDougall clan. Dunstaffnage, whose south wall is solid rock for nearly half its 60 feet height, was used by the kings Alexander II and III in their tremendous and triumphant wars with the Vikings in the 13th century. From Oban, quaint packet boats will take you to the islands, Mull, Colonsay and, of course, Iona where Christianity began in Scotland.

North of Oban the road along the coast passes Castle Stalker, standing upon a minute island in the sea reaches of Loch Linnhe, greatest of the Scottish lochs, and takes you up to Ballachulish Ferry, then branches off

A rainbow curves between these lonely cottages in the Glen Coe district and the two great mountains known as the Shepherds of Etive; Buchaille Etive Mor, 3,345 feet above sea level, and Buchaille Etive Beag, which is a little lower. Mor, with its sheer 1,200-foot rock face, is well known among climbers.

The rounded summit of Ben Nevis (*above left*), at 4,406 feet the highest mountain in the British Isles, looms above Fort William at the south-west entrance to the Great Glen. The west side, which drops like a cliff into the sea, provides one of the most challenging ascents in Britain.

Shipping on the Caledonian Canal (*above*) waits to pass through Neptune's Staircase at Banavie, where eight locks raise the level of the canal 64 feet within one mile. Built by Thomas Telford in the early 19th century, the canal links all the lochs of the Great Glen, creating a waterway over 60 miles long from the Atlantic to the North Sea.

The loneliest countryside in Scotland lies around Sango Bay, Kyle of Durness (*left*) and the 400-foot cliffs of Cape Wrath, just along the coast. The wild, barren hills have never been cultivated and are inhabited only by sea birds and sheep.

to Kinlochleven. South is the pass of Glencoe which always seems grey and overhung with clouds as if to remind you of the dreadful massacre of MacDonalds by Campbells in 1692 instigated by William III. Loch Linnhe goes on narrowing northwards to Fort William under the shadow of Ben Nevis, where begins Telford's spectacular Caledonian Canal that links the Atlantic Ocean to the North Sea at Inverness. This is Glen Môr, the Great Glen, a glorious 60-mile long valley. On its western side opposite Fort William, Loch Eil is a small branch of the Glen that stretches towards Glenfinnann at the head of Loch Shiel. Here, on 19th August 1745, Bonnie Prince Charlie raised his standard and so precipitated his last, dramatic and ultimately catastrophic attempt to win the throne of Scotland.

Beyond Inverness, where each year there is a Highland Gathering, or Games, you come to a part known as Ross and Cromarty, the country of crofters, small landholders who occupy their land under special forms of tenancy, and whose interests, neglected for generations, are now cared for by the Crofters Commission. Beyond this old, double-named county is Sutherland, whose coastline is indented deeply with sea lochs. The most northerly point is a bold headland called Cape Wrath, over 500 feet tall, so named because of the frightful storms that can beat the seas and make navigation impossible. On the way to the Orkney Islands and Shetland Islands is Caithness at the northernmost tip of which is John o'Groats.

Orkney and Shetland belonged for centuries to the Vikings, but were annexed by Scotland in the 1470s. Orkney has Skara Brae, one of the first cluster of stone houses in Europe, over 4,000 years old.

Wales

North Wales

All Wales, like Julius Caesar's 'All Gaul', is divided into three parts – North, Mid and South. North Wales, once Sir (shire) Fôn (Anglesey), Sir Gaernarfon (Caernarvonshire), Sir Feirionydd (Merionethshire), Sir Fflint (Flintshire) and Sir Dinbych (Denbighshire), and now called Gwynedd and Clwyd, is the most mountainous, has the greatest number of Welsh-speaking natives and once contained the principality of Gwynedd which provided more princes as rulers of all independent Wales than any other.

Today, there are several main routes into North Wales, two of them twin roads from Chester, the A55 and the A548. The first takes one past Hawarden where William Gladstone, of Scottish descent, four times prime minister of Great Britain, lived, past St. Asaph, a tiny city of less than 2,000 people and with the smallest cathedral in Britain. A short detour takes you to Rhuddlan, where stand the stark and menacing remains of the great concentric castle built for Edward I in the 1270s. Back on the A55 again to the flourishing sea resorts of Colwyn Bay and nearby Llandudno – the latter with its headland Great Orme's Head, commemorating the crushing defeat in 856 of the Vikings under their leader Horm by one of Wales's super heroes, Prince Rhodri Mawr, ruler of the whole Cymru – through Conwy, site of another massive Edwardian fortress, built in the 1280s, to Bangor, seaport city with a university college and a late mediaeval cathedral built upon the remnants of the first cathedral in Britain, founded by St. Deiniol in 525.

The second route, the A548, skirts the north coast of Clwyd, following perhaps the trail of robber-baron Hugh d'Avranches, Lord of Chester, one of William the Conqueror's three most powerful friends who were given a free hand to try their luck against the independent Welsh. Strong Hugh advanced as far as Bangor where he built a motte-and-bailey castle, but he failed to overwhelm the men of Gwynedd who used their ingrained knowledge of the mountains to hide, spring out and harass him and dash off again – no easy time for a would-be conquering army.

Gwynedd is dominated by the Snowdonia mountain range, now a National Park, the highest peak being, of course, Snowdon, over 3,500 feet high, approachable by a quaint mountain railway or more slowly by a hard slog on two feet, not so high as Scotland's Ben Nevis but thought by some to be sharper and more regal. If you go on from Bangor into Anglesey across Telford's wonderful suspension bridge at Menai, or by train over Robert Stephenson's unusual tubular railway bridge nearby, the mountains follow you all the way across the flat island of Anglesey – Môn, Mam Cymru (Anglesey, Mother of Wales) – home of the princes of Gwynedd who once had a palace at Aberffraw, county of the station with the longest name in the world – Llanfairpwllgwyngyllgogerychwyrndrobwllllantisiliogogogoch (the church of St. Mary in a hollow of white hazel by the rapid whirlpool and St. Tysilio's church near a red cave).

Anglesey is crossed from Menai to Holyhead – where steamers take you to and from Ireland – by the last stretch of Telford's great A5 road from London. This crossed the Welsh border at Chirk on the Salop–Clwyd boundary, and continues through some very lovely countryside, the Vale of Llangollen. On the way look for the magnificent Pont

This beautiful timbered house in Llangollen, Plas Newydd, was the home of the Ladies of Llangollen, Lady Eleanor Butler and the Hon. Sarah Ponsonby. Such was their fame, wit and eccentricity that they had a stream of distinguished visitors, amongst whose numbers were the Duke of Wellington, Sir Walter Scott, Wordsworth and Sheridan.

Conwy Castle, with its 70-foot towers and its 15-foot thick walls, is still in almost pristine condition. Like Caernarvon, Beaumaris, Harlech and several others, it was built by Edward I of England to keep down the Welsh. It is a masterpiece of the Savoyard castle engineer, Master James of St. George, built in four years from 1283 with the pressed labour of 1,500 men.

Cysyllte Aqueduct over the Dee, 1,000 or so feet long on slender, stone piers. Further on is Llangollen Town, where every year an eisteddfod is held for choirs and soloists from all over the world. Llangollen is on the Dee, and on the Llangollen Canal which begins in Horseshoe Falls. The fine A5 forges on into the Cambrian mountains, mile upon mile of rising and falling roadway through wooded valleys and hills, ascending higher and dropping less each time as you edge into the massif and stare in wonder at the awe-inspiring views.

At Bettws-y-Coed, the great road has a south-westerly branch, the A470, and after pausing to enjoy the huge waterfall there, you may take this road to see Dolwyddelan Castle, Welsh-built by Prince Owain Gwynedd and his son, where Llywelyn the Great, his grandson, Prince of all Wales from 1196 to 1240, was born. Go on to Blaenau Ffestiniog, near the Cynfal Falls, source of the famous Welsh slate which, it is said, is so fine that it can be split into pieces one-sixteenth of an inch thick which will bend, and on again past Traws-fynydd where a nuclear power station

Snowdon (*left*) at 3,560 feet the highest mountain in Wales, is seen here from the north west across Llyn Padarn, a narrow stretch of water two miles long, leading into the Llanberis Pass. The only mountain railway in Britain starts from Llanberis, taking passengers on a scenically magnificent trip to a station just below the summit.

The aerial view (*above*) is of the wild, scree-covered summit of Snowdon with Glaslyn, the Green Lake, directly below. The lake's brilliant colour probably comes from copper on its bed – although in Welsh folklore it is said to be bottomless and the home of a sinister monster, the Afanc. Beyond the lake lies the reservoir of Llyn Llydaw in the Gwynant valley.

has been skilfully set into the landscape, then down to Dolgellau, under the shadow of Cadair Idris, a long, precipitous ridge whose topmost peak is almost 3,000 feet high, from which you can see almost all of central Wales. Dolgellau once had gold mines. On the way down, if you can, branch right to Portmadoc from which you can see huge, bleak, lonely Harlech castle, built by Master James of St. George, Savoyard castle-builder on Edward I's payroll, in the 1280s. Harlech was captured by Owain Glyndŵr in 1403 and held for five years against England. Port-madoc is the gateway to the Lleyn peninsula of old Caernarvonshire, with its sea resort at Pwllheli and its interesting castle at Criccieth, half Welsh-built, half English-built and now a ruin.

From Dolgellau south or east you enter Mid Wales, glorious countryside with endless hills and vales. Before you leave North Wales, though, see Bala, about 20 miles north-east of Dolgellau, centre of the 18th-century revival of Welsh non-Conformism, where there is a wonderful lake, the largest natural lake in Wales.

Portmadoc in Caernarvonshire, built during the 19th century at the mouth of the Glaslyn river, is named after William Arthur Madocks, MP. He initiated the reclamation of 7,000 acres of land from the river mouth and then, in 1821, obtained Parliament's consent to the building of the harbour which gives the town its life.

The great road bridge across the Menai Strait (*left*) between the Welsh mainland and Anglesey, a part of Gwynedd, was a major work of the 19th-century engineer Thomas Telford. Carried by massive stone towers, the cast iron suspension bridge has a central span of over 600 feet.

Wales

Mid Wales

Not far from the west coast of Wales and near to Aberystwyth is yet another range of mountains, this one called Plynlimon, with its highest peak reaching to nearly 2,500 feet. Stand upon this summit on a good, fine day and you will be able to see across the whole of central Wales into England. It's not more than 60 or so miles and yet there's a world of difference between one end – West Wales – and west England at the other. Plynlimon overlooks Machynlleth to the north east, small market town where in the early 1400s Owain Glyndŵr, patriot, scourge of the government of Henry IV of England, destroyer of a score of English castles rudely put up in Wales, descendant of the great house of Gwynedd, held his Parliament and declared the independence of Wales, receiving recognition from France and Scotland. On the other side of the mountains, down on the coast, is Aberystwyth, centre of the University of Wales, founded in 1872, and the site of one of the earliest of Edward I's castles. On the hill outside Aberystwyth, in a marvellous position overlooking Cardigan Bay, is the National Library of Wales, which must now, by law, receive one copy of every book published in the United Kingdom.

Twelve miles to the east is Devil's Bridge, a fantastic waterfall enclosed in woods, admired by Wordsworth and Coleridge and described by the 19th-century writer, George Borrow as the 'long, savage, shadowy cleft and the grey, crumbling, spectral bridge', and still one of the truly great sights of Wales. Take the coast road from Aberystwyth south to Cardigan, passing by pretty coastal villages with natural lagoons for swimming, some of them busy, some, like Llangranog, difficult of access and exclusive. Cardigan, former county town of old Cardiganshire, Ceredigion in Welsh, once the name of a separate principality within independent Wales, is hardly more than a village, but it springs to life during the season for

The Elan river (*above, right*) was once a bright stream that splashed and tumbled through a romantic valley which the poet Shelley admired for its loveliness. The stream was then dammed to provide a water supply for Birmingham. The new Elan Valley in Dyfed has a gentler, but no less entrancing, beauty of hill and lake.

At one time the towns of North and Mid Wales, like those of Salop and Cheshire, sparkled with black and white houses. These cottages in Powys (*right*), timbered in large squares with an infill of plaster and whitewashed brick, are probably 200 years old.

salmon fishing in the River Teifi on which it stands.

From Cardigan head east along roads that skirt the lovely Teifi and its long, winding cleft, on the way to Lampeter (Llanbedr), market town with a famous theological college, St. David's, founded early last century. Fourteen or so miles north-west, near the quaint-sounding village of Pontrhydfendigaid, is the Cistercian abbey of Strata Florida. This splendid ruin lies in the Vale of Flowers, Ystrad Fflur, and its monks used to pasture their sheep upon the rich foothills of Plynlimon. Make tracks to the south-east to Llanwrytd Wells, just below the Llyn Brianne reservoir, an inland holiday resort with medicinal springs, and then continue eastwards to Builth Wells, another health resort with chalybeate and sulphur waters, and annual fairs for ponies and sheep. Builth is the permanent home of the annual Royal Welsh Show, where the nation's crafts are exhibited. Builth is a sad town for Welshmen. Not far away their last national ruler, Llywelyn Yr Ail, grandson of Llywelyn Fawr (the Great), was slain by an English

The long shadows of evening fall across rich pastures near Welshpool, Powys, which is the start of the beautiful Severn Valley.

Stunted trees and fine turf mark the sandstone uplands of Brecon which is separated from the Brecon Beacons, the highest mountain massif in South Wales, by the valley of the Usk.

soldier, Adam Frankton, in an ambush during the invasion of Wales by England's Edward I in 1282. Today, a monument on the outskirts of the town commemorates that black day. And north-east of Builth is another spa, Llandrindod Wells, in old Radnorshire (Maesyfed), now part of Powys, notable for its comfortable red brick hotels and guest houses.

About 15 miles south of Builth lies Brecon, once the county town of Brecknockshire (Brycheiniog) and cathedral town of the see of Swansea and Brecon, whose Norman abbey church was raised to cathedral status in 1923. Brecon was once a Roman legionary fort, Y Gaer, among the largest of Roman legionary forts in Britain. It was excavated by that great authority Mortimer Wheeler in the 1920s. Nearby, in the grounds of

Castle Hotel, is Brecon Castle, a Norman shell keep of stone upon an earth mound, with associated buildings, now ruinous, originally put together with stone taken from Y Gaer. Brecon is just north of the beautiful Brecon Beacons.

No visit to Mid Wales is complete without a look at old Montgomeryshire – Trefaldwyn, and now part of Powys. This is a county of contrasts: mountainous on the west where the Berwyn mountains and the Plynlimon range penetrate, and in the east, gently undulating plains where the fields are of great fertility, good for cattle and for crops. It is in fact cattle country. The name Montgomery stems from Roger de Montgomeri, Earl of Shrewsbury, one of the three powerful friends of William the Conqueror who were encouraged by

him to carve out estates for themselves and their associates in Wales. Montgomeryshire contains the source of the Severn, and of the Vyrnwy whose uppermost valley was in the 1890s transformed into a huge lake, about five miles along, to provide water – free of charge – to Liverpool in England, just as, about 30 miles south, the Elan river near Rhayader in old Radnorshire was dammed to make a reservoir for water – also free – for Birmingham.

Mid Wales has in recent years come to the fore in the development of small industry, sponsored with enthusiasm by the Welsh Development Agency which places well-designed factories in some of the towns to provide work for the inhabitants. Newtown is one fine example of their work.

Precipitous cliffs and bold rocks shelter each sandy inlet on this stretch of the Cardiganshire coast, but it is not hard to follow the cliff paths down to reach the delightful, almost private beaches, such as this one at Llangranog.

Wales

South Wales

South Wales conjures up a number of images. Of rugger games and late trains from Cardiff winding their way back through the valleys, filled with men singing their hearts out in that unique, unaccompanied harmony that has made Welsh male voice choirs famous everywhere, grim dust-laden clouds hanging perpetually over row upon row of two-up, two-down cottages, near thundering factories and coal mines, Aberfan – village of tragedy – smothered by an avalanche of black slurry that engulfed a whole school one day in 1966 and took the lives of 116 children. It is all this, but it is much more, too. South Wales has some of the loveliest scenery in all Wales – the views at Symonds Yat are hard to equal anywhere in Britain.

Symonds Yat is in old Monmouthshire (Mynwy) and now part of Gwent, sensible name as it comes from an ancient kingdom there. Gwent borders England. Monmouthshire, an English county from the reign of Henry VIII to 1970, was always Wales and still is, even though few of its natives speak Welsh today. It is hilly country for sheep farming, and the three great rivers, the Wye, the Usk and the Monnow, carve their twisting ways through the landscape, and through fine towns with sturdy houses and clean streets: Monmouth on the Monnow and on the Wye where they join, with its stone bridge which you come upon suddenly after a long descent from the hills, where Lady Shelley Rolls, sister of Charles Rolls of Rolls-Royce, presented her wonderful collection of relics of the incomparable Nelson to the town for all to see; Chepstow, on the Wye, the first town in Wales beyond the western end of the new Severn road bridge, possessor in its castle buildings of the oldest stone great tower in Britain, older even than Colchester or the White Tower of London; Abergavenny on the Usk, site of a Roman fort and a Norman castle; and Caerleon-on-Usk, where the II (Augustan) Legion had its principal base in Britain, extending to nearly 60 acres of ground for about 6,000 men, and including an amphitheatre built in the first century A.D.

The Norman Marcher lords secured their hold on the borderland of Gwent in the 13th century with three castles, forming a triangle five miles long on each side. They were White Castle, Grosmont and this four-sided castle, Skenfrith, with round towers at each angle. Nowadays Skenfrith is a peaceful village, frequented mainly by trout fishermen.

The placid waters of the Lower Wye loop their way from Ross-on-Wye past the ruins of Goodrich Castle and on towards Monmouth. This view (*far left*) is from a great rock, 473 feet high, almost cut off by the river's reaches, looking across a landscape of woodlands and meadows to the village of Symond's Yat.

During the 19th century South Wales was subjected to a Great Coal Rush. People crowded into the valleys, hitherto so wild and lonely, and slagheaps appeared everywhere. Nowadays they are being landscaped and blended into the surrounding mountains. This little town of Cwm-parc in the Rhondda Valley (*left*), seen here from Bwlch Pass, has a new, man-made contour to the left.

Monmouthshire leads into Glamorganshire (Morgannwg) now split into three, Mid, South and West Glamorgan – and quite sensibly. This is the industrial heart of Wales, in whose valleys coal and iron have dominated since the 1800s. These valleys, etched through mountain country by a terrace of rivers all flowing south, the Taff, the Tawe, the Ogwr, the Rhondda and the Rhymney, lead into lower, more fertile ground in the Vale of Glamorgan. They have a long history of suffering, exploitation, industrial accident and unemployment, but they have moulded tough-fibred communities which have always risen above adversity and have smoothed the rough edges of their lives with laughter, love and song. The city of Swansea (Abertawe) is in West Glamorgan and is famous for its university college and Mumbles sea resort.

The capital of old Glamorgan is Cardiff (Gaerdydd), which is also the capital of Wales. It is a city of approaching half a million people, with an unusual example of Norman polygonal stone shell keep castle raised inside an old Roman fort. It is the home of the nation's museum, The National Museum of Wales, colleges of the university of Wales, splendid city offices and, on the edge of the city, the mediaeval cathedral of Llandaff, almost gutted in an air raid in 1941 but now rebuilt and dominated by an immensely powerful sculpture of Christ in Majesty by Epstein, mounted above the nave.

Take the coast road from West Glamorgan into old Carmarthen-

shire (Gaerfyrddyn) now absorbed with Pembrokeshire into the new and appropriately named Dyfed. Carmarthen town, centre for the county's livestock fairs, whose member of Parliament for several years between 1966 and 1979 was Plaid Cymru president, Gwynfor Evans, is picturesque and full of character, with old narrow streets criss-crossing wider modern ones. There are houses in and near Carmarthen where some people speak Welsh as a first language, and even a few who speak no English at all!

Cardiff did not become the capital of Wales until 1955, but it already had one of the finest civic centres in Europe in a spacious, park-like setting. The City Hall, dominated by a clock tower 194 feet tall and a great dome topped by a fiery Welsh dragon, was opened in 1905. The fountains and pool in front commemorate Prince Charles's investiture as Prince of Wales in 1969.

Carry on the coast road to old Pembrokeshire (Penfro). Pembrokeshire was quickly overrun by the Normans in the 11th and 12th centuries who settled there to enjoy the

The cathedral city of St. David's, Pembrokeshire (*right*) is little more than a village. When visitors go in search of the famous cathedral they can hardly find it, for the massive, yet squat medieval building, named after the Welsh patron saint, fits snugly into a hollow. Its walls, built with local sandstone, have an unusual purplish tinge.

Brown-backed guillemots nest all over the bare pinnacles of the pillar-like Stack Rocks (*above*), less than a stone's throw from the limestone cliffs of Pembrokeshire (Dyfed). The rocks are known locally as the Eligugs, perhaps in imitation of the guillemots' call.

rugged, indented coastline, the warm climate and the hills. Pembrokeshire is full of castles which were, it is to be remembered, no more than private fortified homes for lords and knights that made up the Norman armies, and many happy hours can be spent today scrambling among the remains of those that are open – and there are many: Haverfordwest, which guards the town, Tenby, with its associated town walls and Five Arches Gate, Manorbier, home of Gerald of Wales, scholar and historian who served England's Henry II with perhaps too much zeal for a patriotic Welshman, and great Pembroke itself, whose 80-foot tall cylindrical great tower, with walls almost 16 feet thick in places, defeated all attempts to dismantle it, where Henry Tudor, Henry VII of England, Wales and Ireland, was born. It had been built by William the Marshal, friend of King John, and one of the wisest of 13th-century English statesmen. Pembrokeshire also has St. David's, little city on the extreme westerly edge, with a great cathedral founded by Wales's patron saint, built largely in the Middle Ages and now the biggest church in Wales. Inside the nave looks precarious with its pillars that lean away from the vertical, but it is quite safe. Set in a hollow, St. David's is a marvellous sight.

The lovely seaside town of Tenby, built in the shelter of Carmarthen Bay, became a popular resort in the 19th century. Terraces of elegant Georgian villas climb the cliffsides, overlooking sandy beaches and the busy harbour. The ruins of an ancient castle stand on the headland and the main part of the town is surrounded by a medieval city wall.

The view from the coast road leading north from Belfast is among the loveliest in Europe. From Larne to Cushendall, then on towards Benbane Head, the road runs close to the sea with the glorious Glens of Antrim opening out to the west. This group of cottages, hardly large enough to be called a village, is situated at Port Braddon near a salmon fishery.

This little fishing town of Port Stewart in County Londonderry (*right*) used to be called Port-na-Binnie-Uaine — the Port of the Green Headland — and that's just what it is. The fine views, the sea warmed by the Gulf Stream and the sandy beaches make this sheltered town a pleasant holiday spot.

This great neo-classical building at Stormont (*below*), six miles outside Belfast, was given to the people of Northern Ireland by the British Government in 1932 as a home for their Parliament.

ducing areas. A city of shipbuilding (run down now but by no means extinct), aircraft production and cigarette manufacturing, its Victorian and Edwardian public buildings are sometimes ostentatious but nonetheless imposing, like Queen's University (built in Tudor style), City Hall (in Edwardian baroque style) in Donegall Square, Ulster Hall and the College of Technology. Edward Carson, who brought partition to Ireland, lies buried in Belfast's St. Anne's cathedral which, begun in 1898, has been continued in a number of varying styles.

From Antrim cross into County Londonderry, whose county town,

Londonderry – sometimes called Derry for short – is a busy sea-port town on the mouth of the River Foyle. St. Columba founded a monastery here in the 540s, in an oak grove, or *Dhoire* – hence the name Derry. It has two cathedrals, a college and many industries, but its greatest claim to historical fame is the heroic defence its Protestant people put up in the siege of the town by James II in 1689. For 105 days under the command of Major Baker, the defenders endured terrible privations, feeding on horse flesh and when that was gone, dogs and cats, because Protestant relief ships could not deliver supplies.

The Giant's Causeway in County Antrim is one of the geological wonders of the world. Cliffs between 200 and 360 feet high form a backdrop to a fantastic collection of over 40,000 hexagonal basalt pillars, which were formed by the slow cooling of a lava flow. Some are tall, climbing almost to the top of the cliffs; others form a tesselated pavement through the sands, which eventually emerges at Staffa on the Isle of Skye.

What ruins could be more romantic, or more perilously sited, than those of Dunluce Castle, near Portrush, County Antrim? In 1639, part of the 13th-century castle fell into the sea, carrying eight people with it. Not long after, it was deserted and left to crumble away.

The Republic of Ireland

Dublin and the East

You can fly to Ireland from Britain, but it is a hundred times better to travel the more leisurely way, on the sea services from Liverpool or Heysham or Holyhead, the Liverpool run taking you direct to Dublin, the other two putting you down at Dun Laoghaire. As you come across the Irish Sea to Dublin Bay, you see in one tremendous panorama the landscape of Dublin county, low lying for the most part, but on the southern edge the peaks of the Wicklow mountains, rising to the county's topmost peak, Kippure, nearly 2,500 feet. What strikes you is the green, a kind of green you do not see anywhere else – except in other parts of Ireland. This first view of Erin's Isle, so called in ancient Irish poetry and thought to stem from the Roman name, *Hibernia*, is but a microcosm of the Ireland that is to come, for it is a central lowland enclosed for most of its sides by broken hills and mountains, with marvellously soft and romantic scenery.

Dun Laoghaire is the gateway to Dublin. There is an irony about this 18th-century capital of Ireland. It was built by the English upon the nucleus of a far, far older town – Baile Atha Cliath, Gaelic-Irish for village of the hurdle ford – a town actually founded by Vikings who settled in the district under Olaf the White in the 870s, when great Alfred of England was thrashing their kinsfolk in the West Country, and Rhodri Mawr of Wales was chasing them out of Gwynedd. The Vikings called it Dubh Linn, or Black Pool. In 1014, a century and a half later, Ireland's greatest of all kings, Brian Boru, Ard Ri (High King), Taker of Tributes, defeated the Dublin Vikings at Clontarf, a mile or two to the north-east. It was a crushing victory though he fell in battle. It dashed

forever Viking hopes of dominating Ireland. Brian was one of Ireland's two heroes that tower over all the others: the other is Michael Collins – and we shall meet him again.

Dublin is Georgian, beautified with grand public buildings and terraces of houses such as you can see in Bath or Brighton, symbols here of the English Ascendancy, hiding and disguising the terrible slums of the native Irish people behind. Small wonder that the 1916 Uprising, the crucial event in Ireland's long struggle for independence, should have been fought out in Dublin. The city is cut in half by the River Liffey, along whose banks, or nearby, some magnificent buildings stand, notably the Customs House, the City Hall, the Bank of Ireland and the Four Courts. The Liffey is crossed by several bridges, greatest of which is O'Connell Bridge, extension to splendid O'Connell Street, named after Daniel O'Connell who, in the early 19th century, fought in England's Parliament for Catholic rights to vote and stand for parliament, and won.

North-west of Dublin county is county Meath, flat and fertile, whose county town is Trim, with a fine Norman castle beside the River Boyne. Travel north-eastwards along the valley of the Boyne towards Drogheda, passing on the way, about three miles from the town, the site where in 1690 Protestant Dutch William (III) defeated his father-in-law, exiled Catholic James II, who had fled from England in 1688 and now sought to regain his crown with the help of Irish forces. On to Drogheda, now a busy seaport town, major centre of English rule in Ireland during the Middle Ages, and scene of the massacre in 1649 when Cromwell put to the sword the royalist garrison during the Civil

O'Connell Street, Dublin is a graceful boulevard with trees and statues down the centre. At the junction of the street and this unusual bridge over the river Liffey, which is wider than it is long, stands a monument to Daniel O'Connell, who won emancipation for Irish Catholics in 1829.

The Four Courts on the bank of the River Liffey is one of the most imposing of Dublin's many 18th-century buildings. The colonnaded dome rises above a great circular hall from which entrances lead away to the old Exchequer, King's Bench, Chancery and Common Pleas courts, now the home of the Irish Law Courts.

War. In Meath is market town Kells, once home of the ancient kings of Ireland, site of a monastery St. Columba founded in the 6th century, whose famous illuminated book of the Four Gospels, the Book of Kells, now rests in Dublin's Trinity College.

South of Meath is county Kildare, with the sandstone Red Hills and the famous Bog of Allen, a vast expanse of bogland whose peat industry is now being developed with renewed enthusiasm, and scattered all over the gardens of Britain. In the north is Maynooth, where St. Patrick's College has been training Irish Catholic priests since the 1790s. To the west of Kildare is the charmingly named Offaly, edged on its west by the Shannon, Ireland's longest river, and graced with the Slieve Broom mountains, one of the loveliest stretches of inner Ireland.

On the south-east side of Kildare is county Wicklow, dominated by the Wicklow mountains, the tallest reaching to over 3,000 feet, with its lead and copper mining, and the oak and conifer forest round the town of Shillelagh that gave its name to the famous knobbly Irish oak stick meant for walking but more frequently used for fighting. Down to Wexford county, good farming countryside with mountains in the north-west.

Three Celtic High Crosses at Monasterboice, County Louth, commemorate early Christian Ireland. The finest is the 10th-century Muiredach's Cross (*left*) carved with Biblical scenes which are still fresh and visible today.

Cottages are similar all over Ireland; one storey high with two rooms, a thatched or slate-covered roof and whitewashed walls of dry stone. Beyond these typical cottages Lacken Reservoir in County Wicklow (*above*) stretches away into the distance.

The Republic of Ireland

Connaught and Donegal

The central plain of Ireland stretches from Dublin county right across to Galway and Mayo counties on the west coast, and down into coastal county Clare whose southern and eastern inland border is the great River Shannon. On the north bank of the Shannon, a few miles west of Limerick, is Bunratty Castle, seat of the kings of Thomond, whose family name was O'Brien, descendants of Brian Boru. Clare is not rich countryside, despite its plains, but it is very beautiful, with a coastline of cliffs of red sandstone that fall sheer and almost perpendicularly into the sea. In the north of this county is the desolate range of Slieve Aughty mountains. Cross these and you are into Galway county, which is in the province of Connacht (anglicised as Connaught). Heading westwards you come upon a vast lowland plain with bogland, edged on the west by a huge inland lake, Lough Corrib, the second biggest in Ireland (Lough

There is no Irish medieval fortress to compare with Bunratty Castle in County Clare (*left*) which dominates the mouth of the River Shannon. Built in the late 15th century, the solar, dungeons and magnificent Great Hall have recently been restored and furnished.

Neagh in Ulster is the first), up to 150 feet deep in places, with many tiny islets and a band of land at the top separating it from Lough Mask. Corrib was described with style and gusto by Sir William and Lady Wilde in a guide that can still be read. They were parents of the distinguished Irish playwright and poet, Oscar Wilde, whose incomparable wit was at its funniest when he mocked the established institutions of the English society which in the end revenged itself upon him by destroying him.

To the west of Lough Corrib is Connemara, a wild, sad and austere expanse of hills and moorlands, lakes and bogs, flanked by The Twelve Pins, a group of mountains under whose shadow are quarries of stone and of fine Connemara marble, gloriously distinctive in its rich hues of green, used to decorate buildings all over Britain, such as the chancel floor

This stony landscape near Kilkieran, County Galway (*above*) is typical of Connaught and the west coast. Although the climate is mild, the soil is shallow, and the Irish-speaking farmers supplement their incomes by lobster-fishing and collecting seaweed.

at Peterborough Cathedral, and pillars in St. John's College, Cambridge. Galway, the county town, has a university, and a long history of aggravation, for it was almost razed to the ground by Cromwell and it felt the anguish of the war against England in the years 1919–21.

Galway town overlooks Galway Bay, and at the western mouth of the bay are the three Aran islands, huge blocks of limestone rock, desolate but supporting small populations of sturdy, Gaelic-Irish speaking fishermen and their families, men who brave the waters in their stout curraghs, tarred canvas covered small boats like the coracles of the Welsh in Carmarthenshire and Pembrokeshire waters. The Aran islands are famed for ancient forts and cromlechs, and for early Christian ruins.

North of county Galway is county Mayo, with a long, rugged Atlantic coastline of wild and splendid scenery, and the Nephin Beg range of hills and plains, said to be over 200 square miles in area and without a road or a house anywhere. Watching over this scene of abandonment is Nephin mountain itself, over 2,600 feet tall.

To the north-east of Mayo is county Sligo, county of cattle, coal and copper, whose county town of the same name is justly noted for its abbey ruins. A few miles to the west of Sligo is an enormous heap of stones, over 40,000 tons of them, it is said, which are a monument to Queen Maeve, historical queen of Connacht 1,900 years ago, and a major figure of Irish folklore. Her monument and tomb is but one of the many historic, and prehistoric, mounds and monuments sprawling across the countryside west of the town.

At the extreme north-west of Ireland is county Donegal, a mountainous land swept by Atlantic gales, much of it marsh or bog, with farming centred on livestock, but an area world-famous for Donegal Tweed. Donegal is filled with heather-clad moorland and gentle lakes, and tall mountains, notably Errigal, from which the courageous Irish soldier-painter, Earl Alexander of Tunis and of Errigal, took his title. Forty or so miles to the north-east is the small town of Moville, where that other great Irish soldier, Monty, Field Marshal Viscount Montgomery of Alamein, was born.

Clifden, on the wild and rugged coastline of Connemara, is an important centre for salmon and sea fishing, and the sale of Connemara ponies. Beyond the conical hills known as the Twelve Pins lies America.

Muckish Mountain looms above the wild
and beautiful moorlands around
Dunfanaghy in County Donegal, the north-
west corner of Ireland and the northernmost
county of the Republic.

This lonely farmstead lies amid the magnificent scenery around Ballyness Bay in County Donegal. Here the waters of the Atlantic, warmed by the Gulf Stream, surge deep inland across the white, sandy beaches.

The Republic of Ireland

The South West

The luxuriant, almost tropical beauty of the south west is seen here at Glengarriff, County Cork (*far right*), a well-known holiday village nestling in a deep inlet off Bantry Bay. A short boat trip away is Ilnaculin, sometimes called Garinish Island, which has an outstanding formal garden laid out in Classic Italian style.

In the Middle Ages, Cashel in County Tipperary was an important ecclesiastical centre, with a mass of medieval church buildings crowded on to its famous rock. Below, on the plain, lie the picturesque ruins of Hore Abbey. Originally a Benedictine foundation, the abbey was converted for the Cistercians by the Archbishop of Cashel in 1272.

The fourth of the old kingdoms of Ireland is Munster, now the counties of Waterford, Tipperary, Cork, Kerry, Limerick and Clare. For the most part it is mountainous or moorland, with a rugged rocky coastline and a climate that is warmer than anywhere else in Ireland, almost subtropical on good, summer days. Yet it is contrasting countryside. Tipperary has the Golden Vale in the west, probably the most fertile land in Ireland, fringed by hills, producing marvellous dairy farming. In the north is Nenagh, where stands a 100-foot tall cylindrical castle tower, about 55 feet in diameter at the base, which is Norman built except for the later top storey. Nearly 30 miles by road south-eastwards is Cashel, small town beside the celebrated Rock of Cashel, a mass of limestone rock over 100 feet high above the plain. Here, Cormac, 4th-century king of Munster, had his capital and here, in 977, Brian Boru was crowned king. On the top of the rock are the remains of the 13th-century cathedral that replaced the earlier church where in 1171 most of the bishops of Ireland swore fealty to England's Henry II – and thus abandoned the independence of their country.

In the south are the Knockmealdown mountains, once filled with wolves' lairs and eagles' nests, and beyond, just before you cross into

county Waterford, is Clonmel, centre for local trade and birthplace of Laurence Sterne (of *Tristram Shandy* fame), where Anthony Trollope, the 19th-century novelist, once worked as a civil servant. On into Waterford and down to the county town of the same name, once centre of the famous glass-making industry and still producing it.

West of Waterford county is county Cork, the largest in the Republic, whose irregular coastline is cluttered with bays and harbours, notably Bantry, Cork and Kinsale, across whose central plain the Boggeragh mountains streak, flanked by ridges and valleys, and fissured by rivers in parallel – the Blackwater, the Lee and the Bandon. South-east, some 15 miles inland from the sea, is the capital, Cork city, a port with four miles of harbours, an episcopal see, a university town, and the city many Irish people mean when they talk of the 'big city'. Cork lies on the Lee which, as it comes in from the south-east divides into two branches and etches its way through. This fine city rises out of a 9th-century Viking settlement beside the 6th-century monastery of St. Finhbarr. It developed early on a spirit of independence. Not for nothing did the Anglo-Normans call it The Rebel City, for it resolutely defied English authority after the Norman robber barons took

The graceful lines of St. Colman's Cathedral, built of Dalkey granite and decorated with Irish marble, dominate the peaceful harbour of Cobh, known originally as the Cove of Cork.

All over the Dingle Peninsular in County Kerry, which stretches 30 miles into the sea, there are beehive huts, or clochans, dating back to the early Christian period. Most of these are only 3 or 4 feet high and were probably hermit's cells, but this one, the Gallarus Oratory, is 18 feet long and 16 feet high. It was built by corbelling, that is, by setting each course of dry stone to overlap the one below until an arch is formed.

The simple, unchanged life of Old Ireland. A cottager in Bunaw, County Kerry, cultivates small fields and brings in peat and hay with the help of his friendly horse (*far right*).

it in the 1170s. And when, nearly 750 years later, Ireland was once more fighting to be free, two of its lord mayors, Thomas MacCurtain and Terence MacSwiney, gave their lives in the cause.

Along the coast of Cork Harbour is Cobh, an important seaport town with a remarkable 19th-century cathedral in Gothic style, built by Pugin, whose spire reaches to over 300 feet.

West of Cork is some of Ireland's most dramatic scenery. Head for Clonakilty on the south coast. A few miles inland is Woodfield, small village where Michael Collins, organizer of victory against the British and their terrible Black and Tans in 1919–21, and the most celebrated Irishman since Brian Boru, was born in 1890. Thirty-two years later, this much-loved hero, the 'Big Fellow' as

he was known, was assassinated in an ambush on 22nd August, 1922 by disgruntled republicans unhappy about the 'freedom to win freedom' he had obtained by the 1921 Treaty with Britain – shot and killed at Bealnabla, only a few miles from his birthplace. It was Collins who, when asked by an American if the Irish were a great people, replied that they were the greatest people on earth.

The most westerly part of Southern Ireland is county Kerry, whose sharply indented coast is washed by the Gulf Stream and sheltered from the east by the highest mountains in Ireland, the McGillycuddy's Reeks, whose topmost peak is 3,414 feet high. Nearby are the lakes of Killarney, the most famous beauty spot in Ireland, with their trees and rare flowers set against the background of the mountain heights.

Motorways and Main Roads of the British Isles